SCHOLASTIC

LITERACY PLACE®

Imagine That!

Copyright acknowledgments and credits appear on page 128, which constitutes an extension of this copyright page.

ISBN 0-439-06143-1

5 6 7 8 9 10   09   05 04 03 02 01 00

TABLE OF CONTENTS

Imagine That!

THEME

Imagination lets us look at things in new ways.

UNIT 4

Imagine That!

THEME
Imagination lets us look at things in new ways.

www.scholastic.com

Visit the kids' area of **www.scholastic.com** for the latest news about your favorite Scholastic books. You'll find sneak previews of new books, interviews with authors and illustrators, and lots of other great stuff!

UNIT 4

Welcome to

LITERACY PLACE

Imagine an Artist's Studio

Imagination lets us look at things in new ways.

7

Chicken Pedro opened the garden gate.
"What a nice morning!" he said.
"I am going for a walk."
And hip hop, hip hop, off he went.
Hip hop, hip hop down the lane.

9

Chicken Pedro went down the lane
all the way to the big blue lake.
He stopped under the shade
of the lemon tree.
Zum! A large lemon hit him on the face.

Chicken Pedro picked up the lemon.
"Oh my! Oh my!" he cried.
"The sky is falling.
The sun hit me on the face.
I must tell the King!"

And hip hop, hip hop, off he went.
Hip hop, hip hop down the lane.
He soon came across Daniel Duck.

"Chicken Pedro, where are you going
with such a sad face?" asked Daniel Duck.

"The sky is falling.
The sun hit me on the face.
I'm on my way to tell the King!"

"I will go with you," said Daniel Duck.

And hip hop, hip hop, off they went.
Hip hop, hip hop down the lane.
They soon came across Maria the Hen.

"Chicken Pedro and Daniel Duck,
where are you going with such sad faces?"
asked Maria the Hen.

"The sky is falling.
The sun hit me on the face.
We're on our way to tell the King!"
said Chicken Pedro.

"I will go with you," said Maria the Hen.

And hip hop, hip hop, off they went.
Hip hop, hip hop down the lane.
They soon came across Raymond the Rooster.

16

"Chicken Pedro, Daniel Duck, and Maria the
Hen, where are you going with such sad faces?"
asked Raymond the Rooster.

"The sky is falling.
The sun hit me on the face.
We're on our way to tell the King!"
said Chicken Pedro.

"I will go with you," said Raymond the Rooster.

17

And hip hop, hip hop, off they went.
Hip hop, hip hop down the lane.
They soon came across a cave.
And in front of the cave was Rocky Fox.

"Chicken Pedro, Daniel Duck, Maria the Hen,
and Raymond the Rooster, where are you going
with such sad faces?" asked Rocky Fox.

"The sky is falling.
The sun hit me on the face.
We're on our way to tell the King!"
said Chicken Pedro.

"I know a shortcut," said Rocky Fox.
He licked his lips.
"Come through my cave. I will take you
to the palace."

"Thank you, Rocky Fox," said Chicken Pedro.
"You are very clever, but we have wings."
And flapping their wings, off they went.
Flying, flying above the cave.

They flew above the palace gates. They
found the King and Queen in the garden,
sitting under the shade of a green umbrella.

"Why do you all have such sad faces?"
asked the King.

"The sky is falling.
The sun hit me on the face.
We came to tell you!" said Chicken Pedro.
And he handed the large yellow lemon
to the King.

The Queen laughed: "This sun is a lemon!
Let's make lemonade."

The King said: "If we have lemonade
we will also have cake!
Let's bake a cake!"

22

The King brought the cake on a large plate.
The Queen served the lemonade.
Chicken Pedro, Daniel Duck, Maria the Hen,
and Raymond the Rooster ate cake
and drank lemonade.
And they all had wonderful smiles
on their faces.

Lemonade Recipe

4 cups water

12 tablespoons lemon juice

12 tablespoons sugar

1/4 teaspoon salt

Add twelve tablespoons of lemon juice to four cups of water. Add twelve tablespoons of sugar and a quarter teaspoon of salt to the lemon juice and water. Stir well.

Think About Reading

Think about Chicken Pedro and the Falling Sky. Finish each sentence on another piece of paper. Draw a picture to go with each sentence.

First Chicken Pedro met _____ .

Next Chicken Pedro met _____ .

Then Chicken Pedro met _____ .

Then Chicken Pedro met _____ .

Last Chicken Pedro met _____ .

Write a Recipe

What do you like to eat? Write a recipe for your favorite food. Write a list of all the things you need to make the food. Then write how to make it.

Peanut Butter and Jelly Sandwich

- peanut butter
- grape jelly
- 2 pieces of bread

Put peanut butter on one side of one piece of bread. Put jelly on one side of the other piece of bread. Put peanut butter side of bread against the jelly side of the other piece of bread. Now you have a sandwich!

Literature Circle

Why do Chicken Pedro, Daniel Duck, Maria the Hen, Raymond the Rooster, and the King and Queen make lemonade? What else could have fallen from a tree and hit Chicken Pedro on the head? What could he and his friends have made to eat from it? Talk about your ideas.

Author Alma Flor Ada

Alma Flor Ada has been writing books for children for a long time. She writes poetry and stories for children. Some of her stories are written in English and in Spanish. You can learn another language when you read them!

More Books by Alma Flor Ada

- My Name is María Isabel
- Dear Peter Rabbit
- The Great-great-granddaughter of La Cucarachita Martina

The Night Sky

Written by Alice Pernick

Illustrated by Lisa Desimini

SCHOLASTIC

When the sun sets at the
end of the day, the night sky
begins to twinkle and shine.

There are many things to see
in the night sky.

29

The moon is the brightest light in the night sky. Sometimes the moon looks full and round.

Sometimes the moon looks thin and curved. It looks different at different times of the month.

Millions of stars twinkle in the night sky. Some look brighter than others. Some look blue and some look white.

Groups of stars that
form patterns in the sky
are called constellations.

Little Dipper

Big Dipper

Some of the brightest points
of light in the night sky are
planets. They look like stars,
but they do not twinkle.

Look at the sky just before
the sun rises. You might see
Venus shining brightly in
the east.

Venus

Comets blaze across the sky.
They look like stars with long
tails. Comets don't pass by
often. If you see a comet,
it's your lucky night!

Tips for Watching

the Night Sky

Go out on a night when the
moon is not bright.

Pick a spot where buildings
and trees won't get in the way.

Close your eyes and get used
to the dark.

Open your eyes and look up.
What do you see?

Twinkle, Twinkle Little Star

Twinkle, twinkle, little star,
how I wonder what you are.

Up above the world so high,
like a diamond in the sky.

Twinkle, twinkle, little star,
how I wonder what you are.

Think About Reading

1. What is the brightest light in the night sky?

2. What makes the night sky twinkle and shine?

3. What is the name of one constellation in the night sky?

4. Why would you be lucky to see a comet in the night sky?

5. Do you think that a star looks like a diamond in the night sky? Why or why not?

Write a Caption

The Night Sky tells facts about things in the sky. Draw your own picture of the night sky. Write a sentence to go with your picture. Include facts that will help people understand your picture.

Literature Circle

Think about what is in a night sky. What do you most like to see there? Why? Share your ideas.

Illustrator
Lisa Desimini

When Lisa Desimini was a child, she liked to look at the moon and the stars. She still likes looking at the night sky. That's why she was so happy to draw the pictures for The Night Sky.

More Books Illustrated by Lisa Desimini

- How the Stars Fell Into the Sky

- In a Circle Long Ago: A Treasury of Native Lore From North America

I had a million toys, but I was bored.

So I climbed into the attic.

48

The attic was empty.

Or was it?

I found a family of mice . . .

. . . and a cool, quiet place to rest and think.

I met a spider and we made a web.

I opened windows to other worlds.

I found an old flying machine

and I made it work.

I went out to look for someone

to share what I had found . . .

. . . and I found a friend I could talk to.

My friend and I found a game that could

go on forever, but it was time for dinner.

So I climbed out of the attic, and
told my mother where I'd been all day.
 "But we don't have an attic,"
she said.

I guess she doesn't know
about the attic.
She hasn't found the ladder.

BY MYSELF

by Eloise Greenfield

When I'm by myself
And I close my eyes
I'm a twin
I'm a dimple in a chin
I'm a room full of toys
I'm a squeaky noise
I'm a gospel song
I'm a gong
I'm a leaf turning red
I'm a loaf of brown bread
I'm a whatever I want to be
An anything I care to be
And when I open my eyes
What I care to be
Is me

Think About Reading

1. Why does the boy climb into the attic?

2. Does the boy open real windows or make-believe windows in the attic? How do you know?

3. What kind of friend would you want to find in the attic?

4. How can the boy help his mother find the ladder to the attic?

5. How do you think the boy in <u>In the Attic</u> and the girl in "By Myself" are the same?

Write A Postcard

Help the boy in the story make a postcard to tell a friend about the attic. Draw a picture of something the boy saw or did in the attic. Then write about the picture and what the boy saw or did.

Literature Circle

Both In the Attic and "By Myself" tell about kids playing alone. What do you like about playing alone? What do you like about playing with friends?

Author
Satoshi Kitamura

Satoshi Kitamura grew up in Japan where he learned to speak, read, and write Japanese. Now he lives in England, where he speaks, reads, and writes in English. In any language, pictures help make a story such as In the Attic come to life.

More Books Illustrated by
Satoshi Kitamura

- Angry Arthur
- A Boy Wants a Dinosaur
- Sheep in Wolves' Clothing (He's the author, too.)

A DELL YOUNG YEARLING

Starring
First Grade

Miriam Cohen
Pictures by Lillian Hoban

AWARD WINNER

"First Grade has been asked to put on a play
for the school," the teacher said. "Which
story should we do?"

Everybody wanted "The Three Billy Goats Gruff,"
especially Danny. He said, "I want to be the
biggest goat that knocks off the troll's ears!"

The teacher picked Paul to be the troll, and
Danny to be the biggest billy goat. She picked
Sara and Margaret to be the other two goats.
"We will have to make up more parts so
everyone can be in the play," she said.

Anna Maria said, "We could have a little
girl snowflake that dances. I'm the only
one that knows how to do it, because
we have snowflakes at my dancing class."

Danny said, "*No* snowflakes!"

But the teacher said Anna Maria could be one.

"We need some trees to stand by the bridge,"
said the teacher. "Jim, you'd make a good,
strong tree. And George, and Louie, and Willy,
and Sammy too."
"Well, somebody has got to be the trees,"
Willy said to Sammy.

But Jim didn't want to be a tree. He wanted to
be the troll and make awful faces and scare
everybody. He wanted to shout, "Who is going
over *my* bridge?"

They began to rehearse. Suddenly,
the tree that was Jim started singing,
"This Land Is Your Land."
"A singing tree! That's stupid,"
Anna Maria said.

Paul was mad. "He's interrupting me!"
he complained.
"It's not like you to act this way, Jim,"
the teacher said.

Jim didn't sing anymore, but he began telling the others what to do. And he kept telling Paul how to be the troll.

"Make him be quiet!" Paul shouted.

Finally, the teacher said, "Jim, go and sit down."

Jim began talking to himself. "I might not even
be here for the play. I'll probably be going to
Disney World."
Anna Maria heard him. She said, "You're just
making that up."
"You don't know what my father said!"
Jim shouted.

The teacher came over. "Jim, how would you like to be the river that goes under the troll's bridge? You could hide under this blue cloth and move around so it looks like water."

Jim stayed under the cloth and stopped bothering the other actors. But Paul was still mad at him.

After school, Paul said, "You think you're
the boss of everybody!"

He didn't talk to Jim for a whole week,
not even on Friday, the day of the play.

On Friday the school band played as hard
as it could. All the classes marched in.

Soon the auditorium was full of people waiting
for the play to begin. The principal made a long
speech about the play.

Backstage, the teacher whispered,

"Get ready, First Grade. The curtain
is going up in one minute!"

Then the curtain went up. On the bright
stage, the troll waited under the bridge.
The trees were in their places.
The snowflake twirled about near the river.

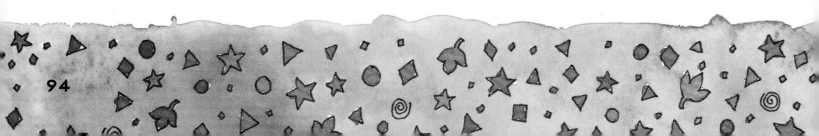

Sara started across the bridge, Trip-trop,
trip-trop. But Paul didn't say anything. He
just stared at the lights and people.

The teacher whispered, "Who is going across my bridge?" But Paul just stared and stared. "He's got stage fright," the people said to each other. It was awful! Nobody could think what to do.

Then the river lumped up and said, "Somebody
is going over your bridge, Mr. Troll. They are
going trip-trop, trip-trop."

"Yes!" shouted Paul. "Somebody <u>is</u> going
across my bridge and they better watch out!
I'll eat them up!" Then they all did their
parts perfectly.

At the end, Danny caught the troll
and knocked off his ears.

Everybody cheered for First Grade.

Their teacher pushed Jim and Paul in front
for a bow.
And they grinned and grinned at each other.

MENTOR

 Read Together!

William Walsh

Muralist

William Walsh uses his imagination to make murals. Murals are large paintings that tell stories.

Everyone chooses the paint for the mural.

The children make sure the mural looks like their sketch.

Everyone has stories to tell. William Walsh tells his stories using paints, brushes, and lots of imagination.

105

Think About Reading

1. What story does First Grade want to act out?

2. Why does the teacher ask Jim to be the river?

3. How does Jim help Paul?

4. Why do Jim and Paul grin at each other?

5. How are the children who put on a play like the children who paint a mural?

★ Write a Poster ★

First Grade wants everyone to come to their play! Make a poster about their play. Tell the name of the play. Tell when and where the play will be, too. Add a drawing to your poster.

★ Literature ★ Circle ★

How do you think William Walsh would like First Grade's play? What do you think he would say to the children after the play?

Author
Miriam Cohen

Miriam Cohen always loved to read! She read while she ate, walked, and even when she should have been doing other things. Still, she didn't start writing her own books until she had children. Many of her books are about Jim and the other children in First Grade.

More Books by Miriam Cohen

- Lost in the Museum
- See You in Second Grade

THE THREE BILLY GOATS GRUFF

A Play by Mike Thaler

Illustrated by Gregory Norton

AWARD WINNER

SCHOLASTIC

CAST OF CHARACTERS

Narrator
The person who tells the story

Little Gruff
The little goat who talks in a soft voice

Middle Gruff
The middle-sized goat who talks in a regular voice

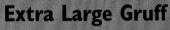

Extra Large Gruff
The extra-large goat who talks in a loud voice

Troll
The bad guy who talks in a mean voice

Sound Effects
The person who makes all the noises

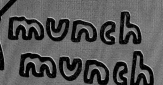

munch munch

Narrator: Once upon a time there were three billy goats Gruff. Little Gruff...

Little Gruff: Hi.

Narrator: Middle Gruff...

Middle Gruff: Hi, hi.

Narrator: And Extra Large Gruff...

Extra Large Gruff: HI, HI, HI!

Narrator: One day they decided to go up the mountain to munch the wonderful things that were growing there.

Little Gruff:	Yum.
Middle Gruff:	Yum, yum.
Extra Large Gruff:	YUM, YUM, YUM!
Narrator:	But to get there they had to cross a bridge.
Little Gruff:	No problem.
Middle Gruff:	No problem.
Extra Large Gruff:	NO PROBLEM!
Narrator:	But under the bridge lived a mean and hungry Troll.

STOMP

STAMP

STEP

Little Gruff:	Oh!
Middle Gruff:	Oh, oh!
Extra Large Gruff:	NO PROBLEM!
Narrator:	No one could use the bridge without going through his Troll booth.
Troll:	I don't charge a dime. I don't charge a nickel. I'll just eat you up like a crunchy pickle.

110

Little Gruff: Oh!

Middle Gruff: Oh, oh!

Extra Large Gruff: NO PROBLEM!

Narrator: So the three billy goats Gruff set off for the bridge.

Sound Effects: Step! Stamp! STOMP!

Narrator:	Little Gruff was the first to arrive. He started to cross the bridge.
Sound Effects:	Step! Step! Step!
Narrator:	Out jumped the Troll!
Troll:	Who's crossing my bridge?
Little Gruff:	It's only me, Little Gruff. I'm on my way to munch the mountain.
Troll:	Well, you have to pay the toll!
Little Gruff:	How much is the toll?
Troll:	I don't charge a dime. I don't charge a nickel. I'll just eat you up like a crunchy pickle.

STAMP STAMP

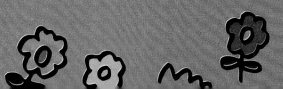

Little Gruff: Oh, don't eat me!
My big brother's coming.
And I have a hunch,
you'll like him better for your lunch.

Troll: Well, okay. I'll wait and eat him.

STOMP
STOMP

Narrator: Middle Gruff was the next to arrive. He started to cross the bridge.

Sound Effects: Stamp! Stamp! Stamp!

Troll: Who's crossing my bridge?

Middle Gruff: It's only me, Middle Gruff. I'm on my way to munch the mountain.

STAMP
STAMP

Troll: Well, you have to pay the toll!

Middle Gruff: How much is the toll?

Troll: I don't charge a dime.
I don't charge a nickel.
I'll just eat you up
like a crunchy pickle.

Middle Gruff: Oh, don't eat me!
My big brother's coming.
And I'm much thinner.
You'll like him better for your dinner.

Troll: Well, okay. I'll wait and eat him.

STEP STEP

Narrator: Extra Large Gruff was the last to arrive. He started to cross the bridge.

Sound Effects: STOMP! STOMP! STOMP!

Troll: Who's crossing my bridge?

Extra Large Gruff: It's me, Extra Large Gruff. I'm on my way to munch the mountain. What's it to you?

Troll: Well, you have to pay the toll!

Extra Large Gruff: No way, Nosey.

Troll: How did you know my name was Nosey?

Extra Large Gruff: Listen Nosey, I've got muscles, and my muscles got muscles. And I know kung fu, karate, and goat jitsu.

Troll: Well, you have to pay the toll anyway.

STOMP!

Extra Large Gruff: Just for laughs, what is the toll?

Troll: I don't charge a dime.
I don't charge a nickel.
I'll just eat you up
like a crunchy pickle.

117

Extra Large Gruff: Cool it, Bridge Breath. If you get in my way,
I'll wrap your feet around your nose,
and you'll spend your days sniffing your smelly toes.

Troll: Now you've got my goat!
I'M COMING UP RIGHT NOW TO EAT YOU UP!

Narrator: So up came the Troll.

Sound Effects: Whack! Whomp! Wrap!

Narrator: And Extra Large Gruff did just what
he said he would do.

Troll: (mumbling) Unwrap me. Phew!
Do my feet smell bad!

Narrator: And then Extra Large Gruff happily went up the mountain to join his brothers for months and months of merry munching.

Sound Effects: Munch! Munch! MUNCH!

All: Snip, snap, snout.
This tale's told out.

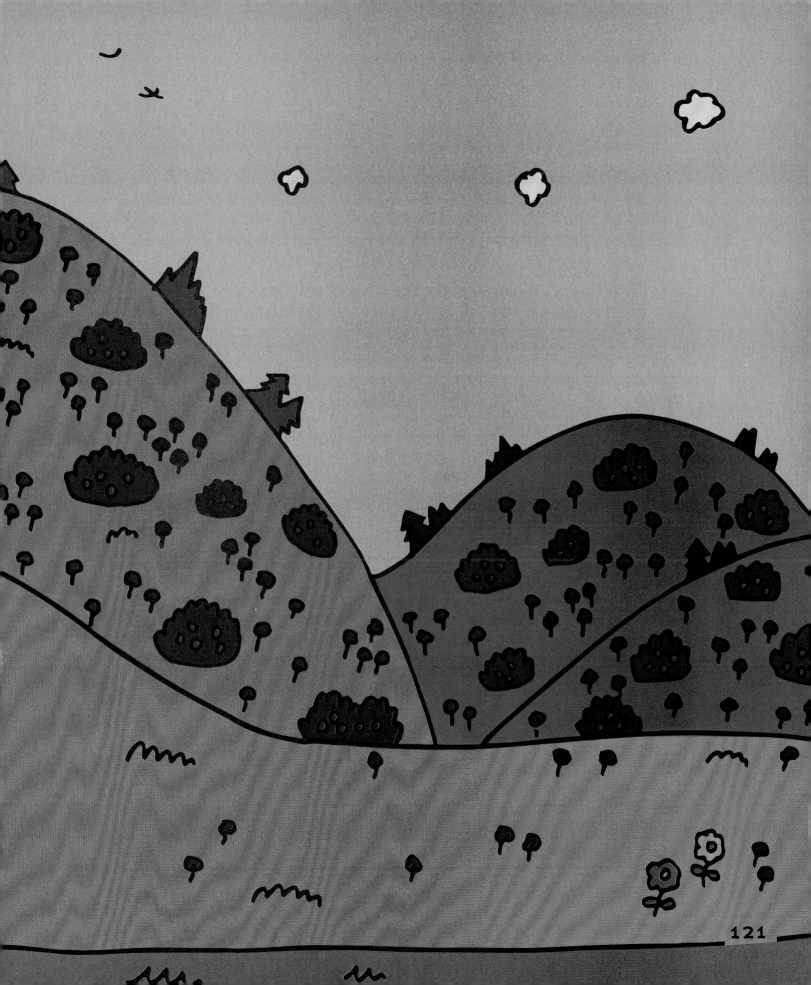

THINK ABOUT READING

Answer the questions in the story map on another piece of paper.

CHARACTERS
1. What are the names of the three goats?
2. Who lives under the bridge?

PROBLEM
3. What do the three goats want to do?
4. What do Little Gruff and Middle Gruff tell Troll?

ENDING
5. How does Extra Large Gruff keep Troll from eating him?

STAMP
STAMP

WRITE A SIGN

What should everyone know about the troll under the bridge? Write a warning sign to put on the bridge. Tell about the mean and hungry troll. Tell about the Troll booth.

LITERATURE CIRCLE

How did the Gruffs feel at the beginning of the play? How did Troll feel? How did they all feel at the end of the play? Talk about your ideas.

TEP STEP

AUTHOR
MIKE THALER

Mike Thaler likes to laugh and make other people laugh. That's why he enjoys writing funny stories for children. He also creates cartoons and draws pictures, visits schools, and helps children tell their own funny stories.

More Books by Mike Thaler

- My Cat is Going to the Dogs

- The Librarian From the Black Lagoon

- Moving to Mars

GLOS

You will find all your vocabulary words in ABC order in the Glossary. This page shows you how to use it.

This is the **word** you look up. →

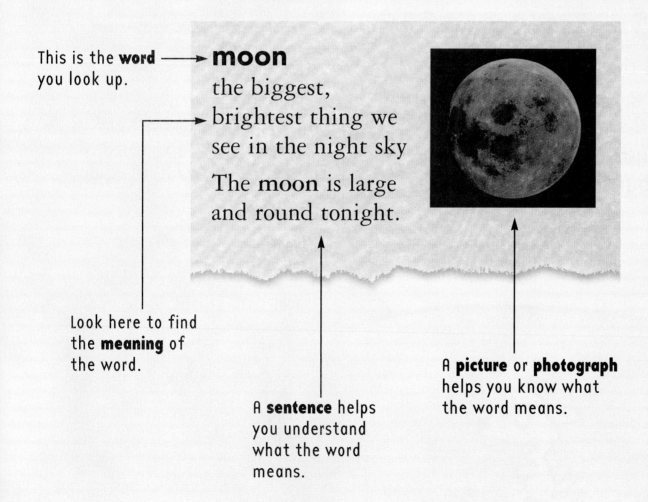

moon

the biggest, brightest thing we see in the night sky

The **moon** is large and round tonight.

Look here to find the **meaning** of the word.

A **sentence** helps you understand what the word means.

A **picture** or **photograph** helps you know what the word means.

actors
people in a play, movie, or TV show

We met the **actors** after the play.

attic
the space or room below the roof of a house

We put old clothes and pictures in our **attic**.

booth
a small enclosed place

Dad paid the man in the ticket **booth** before we saw the movie.

bored
to be tired of or not interested in something

Ben was **bored** with checkers after playing five games.

bridge
something built for people and animals so they can cross over water, roads, and spaces

Cars go over the **bridge** to get over the river.

cake
a sweet, baked food made with flour, butter, eggs, and sugar

Put a candle on the **cake**.

cave
a large hole underground or in the side of a hill

The bear hid her cubs in a **cave**.

dime
a coin that is worth 10 cents

A **dime** is worth the same as two nickels.

first
coming before second

January is the **first** month of the year.

bridge

game

an activity with rules that can be played by one or more people

Our team won the soccer **game**.

goat

an animal with horns, hooves, and a beard

Farmer Brown's **goat** lives in a pen with sheep.

king

a man who rules a country or group of people

The **king** works hard to make the country a better place.

ladder

a set of steps used for climbing

We used the **ladder** to help us hang the pictures.

lemon

a sour-tasting fruit with a yellow peel

Squeeze the juice from this **lemon**.

ladder

light

brightness, or something that gives off brightness

I read by the **light** of my lamp.

lunch

the meal you eat in the middle of the day

Jill and Sandra eat sandwiches for **lunch** at noon.

moon

the biggest, brightest thing we see in the night sky

moon

The **moon** is large and round tonight.

nickel

a coin that is worth five cents

Five pennies equal one **nickel**.

night

the time between sunset and sunrise, when it is dark

Night is the opposite of day.

planets

the nine big, round objects that move around the sun

Earth is one of the nine **planets**.

play

a story that is acted, often on a stage or in a theater

Jack got the part of the hero in our school **play**.

problem

something that is hard to deal with or understand

When I have a **problem**, I ask for help.

shine

to give off light

The moon and the stars **shine** at night.

sky

the area of space high above us

Rain falls from clouds in the **sky**.

stars

faraway points of light that shine in the night sky

We can see **stars** only when it's dark.

story

a tale made up for people to enjoy

My grandfather reads me a **story**.

sun

the big hot ball of gas that gives us light and heat in the sky

The **sun** gives us light and keeps us warm.

talk

to say words

I **talk** to my friends at school.

toys

things to play with

Amber's dolls are her favorite **toys**.

troll

a mean creature in a folk tale who often lives under a bridge

The prince saved the village from the evil **troll**.

Acknowledgments

Grateful acknowledgment is made to the following sources for permission to reprint from previously published material. The publisher has made diligent efforts to trace the ownership of all copyrighted material in this volume and believes that all necessary permissions have been secured. If any errors or omissions have inadvertently been made, proper corrections will gladly be made in future editions.

Unit Opener: From IN THE ATTIC by Hiawyn Oram, illustrated by Satoshi Kitamura. Illustrations copyright © 1984 by Satoshi Kitamura. Reprinted by arrangement with Henry Holt & Co.

"The Night Sky" from THE NIGHT SKY by Alice Pernick, illustrated by Lisa Desimini. Copyright © 1994 by Scholastic Inc.

"In the Attic" from IN THE ATTIC by Hiawyn Oram, illustrated by Satoshi Kitamura. Text copyright © 1984 by Hiawyn Oram. Illustrations copyright © 1984 by Satoshi Kitamura. Reprinted by arrangement with Henry Holt & Co.

"By Myself" from HONEY, I LOVE by Eloise Greenfield. Text copyright © 1978 by Eloise Greenfield. Reprinted by permission of HarperCollins Publishers.

"Starring First Grade" from STARRING FIRST GRADE by Miriam Cohen, illustrated by Lillian Hoban. Text copyright © 1985 by Miriam Cohen. Illustrations copyright © 1985 by Lillian Hoban. Reprinted by permission of Greenwillow Books, a division of William Morrow & Company, Inc.

THE THREE BILLY GOATS GRUFF by Mike Thaler, illustrated by Vincent Andriani. Copyright © 1996 by Scholastic Inc.

Photography and Illustration Credits

Photos: pp. 7br, 102 bl, 103c: Merry Alpern for Scholastic Inc.; p. 27, Courtesy Alma Flor Ada; p. 45, Moya McAllister for Scholastic Inc.; p. 73, Farrar, Strauss & Giroux; p. 105, Donna F. Aceto for Scholastic Inc.; p. 123, Courtesy Mike Thaler.

Cover: Vince Andriani for Scholastic Inc.

Illustrations: pp.2–3, 22–23:Vince Andriani for Scholastic Inc. pp.6–7: Jackie Snider for Scholastic Inc. pp.8–23:Loretta Lopez for Scholastic Inc. p.42:Eileen Gilbride for Scholastic Inc.

Illustrated Author Photos: pp. 27, 45, 73, 105, 123: Gabe DiFiore for Scholastic Inc.